SERIES | INDIA

SERIES | INDIA

Elizabeth T. Gray, Jr.

Four Way Books
Tribeca

For David Shapiro

Please direct all inquiries to:
Editorial Office
Four Way Books
POB 535, Village Station
New York, NY 10014
www.fourwaybooks.com

Library of Congress Cataloging-in-Publication Data

Gray, Elizabeth T., 1952-
[Poems. Selections]
Series | India / Elizabeth T. Gray, Jr.
pages cm
ISBN 978-1-935536-55-0 (alk. paper)
I. Title.
PS3607.R3889A6 2015
811'.6–dc23

2014030216

This book is manufactured in the United States of America and printed on
acid-free paper.

Four Way Books is a not-for-profit literary press. We are grateful for the assistance
we receive from individual donors, public arts agencies, and private foundations.

This publication is made possible with public funds from the
New York State Council on the Arts, a state agency.

NYSCA

and from the Jerome Foundation.

[clmp]

We are a proud member of the Council of Literary Magazines and Presses.
Distributed by University Press of New England
One Court Street, Lebanon, NH 03766

CONTENTS

It can be noted here that…several books have appeared in which the authors, partly unconsciously, but also partly deliberately, have given the impression that they are brothers of the League and had taken part in the Journey to the East.… But they all have nothing to do with the League and our Journey to the East…their journeys were not remarkable and they discovered no new territory, whereas at certain stages of our Journey to the East, although the commonplace aids of modern travel such as railways, steamers, telegraph, automobiles, airplanes, etc., were renounced, we penetrated into the heroic and the magical.

Hesse, Hermann. *The Journey to the East.* Hilda Rosner, tr. New York: Farrar, Straus & Giroux, Noonday Press, 1956. p. 5-6.

I can only say that the wind of the change as it has happened has numbed me, to the point where the false way and the true way are confounded, where there is no way or rather where everything is a way, none more suitable or more accurate than the last, oblivion rapidly absorbing their outline like snow filling footprints. This despite the demonstrable rightness of the way we took, of our emergence into a reality that is perfect. Despite the satisfaction, endless as a sea.

John Ashbery. "The New Spirit." *Three Poems. John Ashbery: Collected Poems 1956-1987.* New York: Library of America, 2008. p. 256.

1   THE CROW

Once upon a time when Brahmadatta was reigning in Benares

a crow pecked to death her fledglings and fled into the forest.

And what to do with the bodies spread out along the muddy bank,

the big leg-pile and lopped-off heads. The rest of the flock,

dismayed, slept that evening by the river in the dark folds of its favorite

   banyan.

Nevertheless, there remained that nagging question,

the monsoon due any day and the emperor camped at Patna.

Had he sent a regiment it would have been too late.

The next morning the King of the Crows, in the course of a progress

   through his dominions,

arrived at the river and there heard the tale from the troubled flock.

You were right, good crows, to neither punish nor pursue, he said.

Every tree will be the one in which she did them in.

See, here are their bangles, said our guide, proudly,

and sure enough there they were, dim in the airless case, flanked by small cards

with date, provenance, and bits of birth story.

The sunlight spread across the pretty kitchen table.

And here is Andrew, Sarah thought, putting down her book, back from market with another allegory.

2   MOTHER I

It will soon be hard for her to do this on her own,

the doctor said, and we wondered how

the all-powerful destroyer and birth mother,

the Vulva of the Ten Worlds, who drinks

from the brainpans of the Deluded,

would handle mechanical assistance and live-in staff.

Prayer, sacrifice, payroll. Maybe not in that order.

A glimmer of it earlier in the year:

the wood-chipper choked, faltered, got so erratic

that even the mechanic barked, "Back off!"

Walk away. Now. While you can. Don't bother

with marigolds on the threshold.

That's what I told them,

didn't I? *Mummy?* The grayscale of everything

made everything easier to see. Just look at her

making her entrance, floating

on the arms of her walker.

3 THE JEWELED DEER

Her mother woke and had to blame somebody

and barked at the nurses why couldn't they—

so much it hurt—and then sent her again—some test

for later this morning—the doctor would just be

interminable Sarah thought bracing herself

to hear it all again. Surely in India there would be,

in a forest of strange trees, a clearing, where he and I

would gather delicate renunciations and become wise

together. When her mother threw books and threatened

to break each vase, out in the hall that thought

shook its slender antlers of ivory, beckoned, and shyly,

dappled in diamond and topaz, disappeared

into a thicket of gurney and wheelchair.

4   UNDER THE BANYAN

Yes, but who knew? Who will go? Monkey demanded

and the rest grew quiet. Out of ideas and urgent. Remember?

The ticket nowhere to be found, thus the rickshaw to the Embassy.

Will the bank wire money? Will Mother buy it all,

authorize it, surprise us? Who will have stood up to her,

who knew, who will go were still the questions.

Then the chattering like mad begins again and what happened

in the end remains one of the myriad root-wisps

we saw in the scented air and from which we learned

nothing at the time. In that life I was Monkey and you

were both the road shrine and crow and this tree

was half the forest it is now.

5 CIRCUMAMBULATION

Against the flat white sky
flat white snow had happened
to the mountain's sharp cols
and fell couloirs.

The small man coming into the valley
after many years of traveling
finds the absence of the longed-for mountain
consistent with the teachings and begins

what, Andrew had asked her.
He in the doorway, she
at the center of the shallow parlor.

6   VISITING

It is put away. That's what she does

whenever I ask her about her time in India.

What did she see? What happened? Why

is the pasta gratinée so cold?

Ask them again, will you dear?

All of my questions, again.

7   ARRIVALS

Stunned and immediate recalibration upon descent into stifling and acrid, holding *Lonely Planet* passport visa Twizzlers backpack *Gita*, clearing immolation and other customs, hacking through dark thickets of limbs and torsos toward taxis, in lieu of inlaid alabaster arch, instead of blue multi-armed god-on-hill, what they come upon curbside are Blake and Edwina late of Nottingham claiming to know reasonable hostels near a brilliant ashram and might one factor in karmic implications and split the fare with them?

8 THE FIRST EVENING, ON THE WAY BACK TO THE HOSTEL

At the end of the stifling lane, broken steps going down to the river.

On the bottom step, an old man facing the river,

wrapped in saffron, holding a copper tray. Above and behind him

a black-haired boy, hips wrapped in white cloth, holding a small, bright bell.

The boy rang the bell and the man

poured liquid onto colored dyes and white flowers at the center of the tray

and placed it at the edge of the thick water. The man

raised his arms above his head, palms together, and murmured a braid of words.

He picked up the tray with both hands and cast the dye and flowers out

onto the zinc surface of the river. The boy rang the bell again,

stepped down the crumbled stairs and broke apart

into a conspiracy of monkeys that snattered loudly,

pinned the old man up against the water, and stole from his stained hands

leftover crumbs from his long words, squabbling over

syllables of *anekashastrahasta* that had sought the silted bar at the center of the river

where a sere tent, lit from within, is, this evening, a beacon

for fishermen, for each leaf-bowl

bearing its tiny lamp out onto the shimmering.

9   SERMON

Because that's how you break through, said Blake.

How you see desire for what it is.

His brown hair was matting nicely, his loincloth

getting the hang of him. He had some chants down pat

and nicely-emerging ribs. Om-most there, he quipped,

striking a pose. The horse's ass-ana, I believe,

said Greg quietly, and we braced ourselves

for another one on the virtue

of sitting still among charred tibias and pariah dogs.

Of trying to keep it hard but not come. Of that

No.

But there must, she thought, why we're, why

we seek the blue-milk sea, the crags of the mighty Vindhyas,

the Tower of the Ten Winds, the thread offered

that we can decline or use.

10   IN THE KITCHEN

She had often painted a crude image of the Goddess—

the bloody lips and fangs, the scepter

of femur, the bleached diadem of skulls—

and cut it into pieces. Whenever she had looked carefully

her mother making dinner seemed just fine.

11   DEVI: THE GODDESS

As Durga, she is difficult of access.

As Parvati or Uma, daughter of the Himalaya.

Also Gauri, the golden one.

And Kali, the black one, or time, when time

is a woman. This is all the same force.

Black against. Cloud and snow, inaccessible

crevasses and couloirs are Nanda Devi,

bliss-giving goddess. Maha Devi, great mother.

Shashti is sixth. Six days after birth

she injures children and before.then must be placated

with fasting, gifts, distractions. The goddess

is here inside me, I can feel her

kick, said poor Gisèle, gaunt and pregnant by the fruit juice stand,

my mother might send money but

I can't reach her.

I am the golden child,

and share my lord's austerities deep in my father's mountains.

Abstinence is the power between us. Gold, black,

prepared to injure, my body

heats the cold wind.

           All of this is

difficult to access, difficult to ask for, like sex,

Latin for six.

12   BANYAN

"This one it is so much like all their god," said the divine Nadia

from Minsk, drawing another analogy out of her string bag.

"Everywhere can see forest but not tree."

But hadn't that single pure core,

unspooled in the *Upanishads*,

been available before, at home:

in snow the thin stand of aspen not hung

with threads and bassinets that will not take root

but end-stopped, luminous, reluctant?

Not a pantheon of one, but each alone?

13   THE DANCE

And then went down to the ship, read Andrew, aloud,

naked to his waist and out the window

fishermen hauled their dhow up the beach.

A letter came, said Sarah, but it won't cohere.

I can never tell what she wants. Hold me.

And so for solace they arrange themselves

and where feet touch floor forth come

sparks and nets, names, shells and ferries,

the flickering gleam in the basket as the baitfish die

and the lame man holding them looks on.

What they had come for, why

they were here and what it meant,

these were sometimes

what they had imagined, with its surrounding

radiance, and sometimes

nothing that could have been imagined.

What they had imagined upon setting out

was what it would mean, why they came,

what in the end hemmed some in.

Why they came and what it would mean,

this that they came for, that had imagined them,

that had imagined them coming and what it would mean

for them and for what came afterwards,

was the finding,

the finding surrounded by radiance, by what was,

despite what had been imagined,

small and mighty and blue.

But what had not been imagined, who

had not been imagined, these also

were waiting for the ones who were destined to come.

These imagined the ones who were coming,

who were destined to come, who

at the moment of their setting out had tried their best

to imagine what was waiting for them, what,

afterwards, in that life, they would say they found.

15   MOTHER II

Once upon a time, after a hundred-year war, all the gods
were driven from the three worlds by the armies of Mahisha
the Great Buffalo Demon. The gods went whining to Brahma
who led them to Vishnu and Shiva.

Brahma bowed low before those Mighty Protectors and said,
"From heaven, earth, and the underworld the Great Buffalo Demon
has cast out all the poor gods you see here.
Even Wealth, Fire, and Death
wander like men aimlessly across the earth."

Shiva and Vishnu went white with rage
and with all the other gods lasered their powers
to a single point in deep space and there
was the Goddess, born
as Durga, *difficult of access*.
And all the gods rejoiced.

"And now your weapons," she said.

And so they relinquished trident, mace, bracelets, discus,

spear, pearls, bell, silks, and beads.

Death handed over his staff.

The sea his conch, and a noose.

Astride her lion, scraping the sky,

churning the oceans, shaking the mountain ranges, the sound

of her bowstring thundering through the three worlds,

she laughed.

She makes short work of Mahisha's army.

When he reveals, for a moment, his true form

she hacks his head off.

From the beginning we believe

she is always there, that there is nothing

she cannot do.

16   EACH OF US HAS OUR DHARMA

Unlike the rest of us Nadia was practicing

attachment. If you were male it was *that's it*

instead of *not this, not that*, it was like

transcendence be damned and every Noble Truth,

as in all four, out the window. Suffering.

How could touching her be anything related to.

Devi's arms and garlands dispel illusion and free

the single-minded devotee, Stan said and the boys agreed.

But Andrew had not seen, or so he said, how her linen bag

pulls the neckline of her tunic off her shoulder

and her glass bangles of many colors chime

in ways I can neither assess nor replicate.

Beyond that there was in her smoky speech an absence

of articles—definite, indefinite—and the men lean in

dying to fill that absence better than.

17   BLAKE WAS TALKING UP A NEW RITE

                              You go alone

to a really scary place spread out your skin cook

your body parts up in your iron pot add specific syllables

summon the demons feed 'em and you're free.

You have to get it just right so he went over

invitees and ingredients again, dandling lung,

aorta, liver, femur, and diphthong. Brad

said nothing but Nadia offered the room a few more inches of arm.

I never have to call them, said Sarah, quietly. Two of them

are always there: an opaque imperceptibly moving surface

that stretches away on every side and betrayal

for which there is no evidence but of which I am

entirely certain. Doesn't love dismember ourselves?

Every curve and secretion offered up?

Afterward you pick up your skin and go home.

it's still dark and cold. Andrew's rib

under her arm his scent the undeniable

fact of him warm and even when he's sleeping

American, holding on for her

to all that loosens its hold:

what she told people when asked

for example the story about before

when we were some kind of bird

beaks buried under the outer layer

of each other's feathers.

19   VARANASI I

Once Shiva, in his rage, cut off Brahma's head

which stuck to His hand. Howling He roamed

but the head held firm.

Thus He is *Kapālin*, skull-bearer.

Here,

where Ganges washes away the sins of a hundred lifetimes,

it fell to earth. This is His place.

The cremation ground He never leaves.

Thus it is *Avimukta*, never-forsaken or never-abandoned.

Here, and between your eyes, in your heart, navel, loins,

at the crest of your skull

here in my hand.

Here, by means of the Grand Trunk Road,

by means of the breath, at the trident of rivers and railways,

in the long shadow of Himalaya.

Even here.

Release is difficult.

Rebirth is horrible.

A man should crush his own feet

with a stone

to stay in Varanasi.

20   AT THE SHORE TEMPLE

Dawn breaks over the Bay of Bengal and waves

cherish the low steps and the statues' broken feet.

Surely this is all. Everything I would share with you

is here at this tide and temple.

Stay with me, Mother. Watch the gulls.

In our other life I will tell you who we were

this morning, here, on this beach.

Ash. Ash is what it came down to. Once upon a time

the Great God sat immobile among pines,

meditating on the *not* in the wood,

and up comes Love, He-Who-Interferes,

the rude intruder pushing up hard toward the mountains' daughter

on the other side of his pants. The way her tunic falls

asymmetrically at her neck

hollows graceful and beckon.

Detach.

Inhabit your breath. Through pines.

Transcend pain in your legs. Train that third eye

for revision, or actually changing how it was,

for incineration.

Kama, the love god,

goaded Him and was cindered. *Mantra interrupt us*

and its consequence. In the cold grove silence.

Here, she comes,

assuming her place beside that whole in the air.

22   IN THE HILLS

it rains us silver
into the gored lane

and I disintegrate you there
thinning among birches

coolly you rise
and set myself on fire

we love myself sparingly
and we carry the loss of me
to a last incline
without flare or fondness
whether we are early or beauty

23   THE GURU

Listen, I am he who tells you:

follow not the person

but the words. If you follow

Buddha, if you follow

Jesus, if you follow

Muhammad, you will

miss him. Listen. Open to me

your body and you open

your soul to joy. So, all

is an offering. This, this is *bhakti*,

devotion, divine. If you follow

the person you will lose your way.

Was that it, wondered Andrew.

The woman in the worn green sari

scrubbing juice stains from the terrazzo

floor, from Syracuse, New York,

thought so. While it had been okay

for sweepers and pyre-makers

to be aloof yet rich

with meaning, blonde Louise

cleaning ashram latrines, green eyes

overflowing with devotion—was this

horrifying or proof?

                                     Samsāra

is our chain of lives, the snarled illusion

of he and she, of multiplicity. That-which-interferes.

    He who sees the many and not the one

    wanders on from death to death.

                                     Ātman

is spirit, soul, thumb-sized chest-flame, what transcends.

So the Upanishad said

          but we were tired

from the hike and picnic, from wandering

aimlessly across the earth. Then the medic from the UN,

over the din of unrestrained children, pointed to the man

right across the aisle with the blue sheen on his skin

dead to the day's extremities. Our edges, too,

were numb, and those little pricks couldn't get to us

like they used to.

Saṃsāra and *Ātman* walk into a bar.

"What'll it be, Sam?"

Another round of gorgeous distractions,

dappled in diamond and topaz.

At the end of her gaudy parade, at the rim

of devotees, the towering Mother,

this broad and gory goddess,

is thrown into the sea. The dense streets delight

and weep. Durga has departed. We are left free of evils

but nonetheless, bereft.

This guy writes pretentious stuff,

said Sarah, coiled on the balcony in Mumbai.

Just clay and mylar.

Lunacy, scapegoat, propitiation.

So put down the book.

That's why we kill our mother and make her image

over and over. To do just that one thing.

26   VISHNU

Lit from behind you stepped from the cloud

of your long shower into our room,

towel pale and catenary across your torso,

and held your palm out to me accepting

my ambivalence as if it were jasmine.

27 THRESHOLD

Blake was always fervent but this

was wholly different, these prostrations imprecise,

pace, sweat, a fetal coil moaning about cold, baffled chanting

isn't going to help here is it

they asked one another in alarm. Too sick

to travel or sick enough to chance it because this

might be the whole deal right here,

incarnate, each of our aspirations like Blake's up on its hill

approached dutifully, the mind *in each step*,

jasmine mangoes and scarves carried carefully toward a grove

in which some god may someday dance

but he's not here. Mother,

what should we do? Hear our prayer.

As if their story were a seed, Ananda,

that fell by chance into some stone niche and nursed

by warm air and rain

spun fine filaments of root to earth

and is the small forest in which they wander.

On the wall in glittering anklets the painted beauties danced.

Self-contained and gossamer. Sarah and Nadia

followed into the disallowed and all that

within their own limbs leapt.

lustrous disheveled wearing nothing her right hands say *fear not* and *here*

is my gift her left hands hold cleaver and severed head black skull-necklace

tangled cloud tornado her face looms laughs gargantuan earrings of dead

children blood-smear through shredded arms sewn skirt shouting terrible

sits on Time's corpse fucks him for us surrounded her jackals burning-

ground and cold cries her face glows lotus her third eye the sun rising

think on Mother Kali and all comes true

he said   the fever was very bad

30   ONE AFTERNOON SARAH GETS LOST
IN THE STREET OF BUTCHERS
THE GODDESS AS DURGA PROMISES BLESSINGS

she thinks *when in a forest*

there were *on a lonely road*

a series of lefts *or surrounded by fire*

before her *when encircled by*

and there were *robbers*

thin men who stole *in a desolate place*

after her and hide *or seized when stalked*

among flayed skins *lions tigers wild elephants*

pale stiffening *imprisoned*

an armless man *with weapons*

imagines her *in dreadful straits*

by stacked *or tormented*

buffalo shins *whoever remembers*

loosening *these deeds of mine*

her clothes *is freed from*

danger

Which god's

Song which song

Is the bronze

God's song

Song is an alloy she longs to be

She pieces together

Petals blends

Orange and yellow

Evening comes

The god is the song

In bronze

32   LATE DECEMBER, IN KERALA

It was Christmas. Someone must remember Jesus, said Thomas,

in the port where his eponymous apostle came ashore.

And he was right: at the top of the fishy lane out of nowhere suddenly

this white church, its starched faithful singing familiar

but unintelligible hymns, where, in Her bright vitrine,

the blue-eyed vermilioned Virgin, wrapped in marigold and saffron,

cradles her pale human-headed two-armed son.

33   HIMALAYA

Go. Summon all the mountains, says Himalaya.
The ash-smeared god wants my daughter.
(At his feet silver river veins, banana leaves, lemons,
trekkers on trails gaping up.)

They come, their faces grim:

Manaslu.

Gasherbrum I.

Dhaulagiri.

The Annapurnas.

K2.

Kanchenjunga.

Lhotse.

These,

that Franz was always going on about, that we'd beheld
from the valley floor where we waited for avalanche sound
to roll over and smother us, that Meissner the crazy German
and some other guy had climbed without oxygen,
can't decide.

It lies with the god and girl.

The sleeping bag between them on the cold floor.

The girl has made up her mind but she's not a god.

Halfway through our time there, it was late

and we were changing trains at Kanpur

when we lost Leo who'd been with us ever since.

It was not even that crowded when we got back

with tea and sweets—he'd been watching the bags

which were where we'd left them but he was not.

It was late. Each of us, it turned out, suddenly missing

something—Veda, pen, pot, scarf,

beads—that seemed, when it went missing, trivial

but became, over time, of vast importance

the way Leo went from quiet guy to lost guide late at night

on the platform in Kanpur when we were changing trains.

What was reliable and in place, what we had come to know,

what, despite being so bizarre as to be beyond imagining when we set out,

had become familiar, had become familiar and turned on us,

on us, not away from us, and Leo was the first to go. It began with Leo.

35   GOING EAST

At some point isn't it just going

west? Follow that Bodhisattva

far enough east and you're back

in some Berkeley, dense with dope

and earnest adherents. That inked

Zen brushstroke, inscrutable

syllables—you should be able

to see that here, he said,

in the calligraphy of scooters,

T-shirt sellers and touts.

The texts here speak

of a thumb-sized flame

in my rib-shrine. But text's

insufficient, cautioned a senior

disciple from Eindhoven.

Such pressure. Everyone

camped by the fig tree

at Bodh Gaya where

Buddha reached *nirvana*, where

the stoned American known

simply as Man said, Don't think

about it so hard. But despite,

he did, and it would not come.

36 ATHEOPHANY

Vishnu has risen

From his bed of serpents

Huge coils of cloud rise up white

From where He lay and shake the sun

From their shoulders

At each frond-root coconuts

Close ranks and the beach

Tries to thicken

The rolling constrictors of the air

Unspool their rain and begin

Their hiss across the sea

We watch with awe

That abandonment come ashore

37   WEARING THIN

Even James had had it with shrines.

If he had to take off those shoes one more time

there would be, he averred, more than just three hells to pay

so we checked into a high-end hotel:

yes absolutely you are from where.

Two Japanese kept taking photos of Shiva's

mossy lingam in the lobby without

first offering the requisite marigolds—

doubtless the blunt stump took notice

and the road back to Kyushu would be strewn

with untended consequences. Nadia

ripped off bits of her grey scarf and wrote out

prayers for something (we were tired of asking)

and went off in search of a banyan.

She's really going to tie one on this time,

Jack said, and we collapsed in laughter as fraught

as the route we saw home in those moments

when you dare to look, when the rains

go into week three and have ceased

to be novel or foreign.

38   SARAH

The trail of shrines was cold.

The god was mute, and stayed put in his shape

asleep next to her.

The backpack is empty and the notebook full,

she thinks and goes to the window

where the city you knew spreads out

into subtle attributes and early morning dark.

In the lanes, engines turn over, someone spits,

headlights come to life. The phone,

stashed in its quiver, waiting.

39 EVENING, ROOF OF THE GUESTHOUSE, PUSHKAR, RAJASTHAN

As the man and woman stand in their jeans holding hands,

looking out at the lake, a pregnant cow in a nearby lane

nuzzles clots of garbage that squabble and scuttle away.

After the man turns, gently removing her necklace, dipping it

in the cistern three times, and after he holds it up against

the backdrop of the town and she steps away,

hands over her mouth, the two waiting crows depart,

leaving him, as she does, standing there

by the pink and yellow saris hung out to dry

in the imperceptible breeze that is, this evening, filled

with a fine dust invisible except as a corona

gilding everything not already in shadow.

40   NADIA, IT TURNS OUT, IS A RIVER

"Can make case for Durga marry Buffalo Demon," said Nadia, plaiting her

   pale hair.

"Very rich, handsome, with army, track record, has real estate of all gods."

Jason thought we had two more weeks of her at least but then she wrapped

   herself

in the Godavari and fled east to where the sea

unraveled her tawny edges into lead and silver, leaving us suddenly

tributaries offering all we had, our wan elixir

leached from villages each with its elders and gods of illness.

We're going to myth her, said Lee to Glen, who had arrived the day before,

from Hyderabad, with Jim.

41   THE EIGHTFOLD PATHS

Over chappatis at the tea stand we heard Bill had moved on:

Bangkok then up to the Buddhist city at Pagan, and Katrina

in Sri Lanka to study Pali near Gal Vihara.

Glenn had gone straight to Japan and Zen:

moss and raked white stone seen from a platform

long-sought antidote to the gaggle of theogonies on offer here.

Absence and insight briefly visible between brush and ink.

The pines at Daisen-in. The stones at Ryoan-ji. Relief

from whatever it is a million ascetics splashing in a river seek.

So on bad days, when stink and chatter arouse the hooded

Cobra of Disillusion, does an exit beckon?

Among black pines along a blank-white ridge wait

cross-legged under thatch for the full moon

to appear and illuminate what has baffled or become hard to bear?

Well, said Alastair, for that you'll have to go East from here.

What we have brought here in our hand

What we have here under our hand will not fall away

It has attached itself it has become

An attachment

An attachment that will never leave

A petal that is not fragile

A bronze marigold, maybe

Something gold falls to earth and rolls away

Something cold falls and rolls away

One thing the one thing that would never leave

Became cold and rolled away when we arrived

Here was where the god brought His great sin in His hand

It followed Him as he wandered

The fell thing followed Him

It was His fell attachment

That never left Him

But when He arrived at the river it fell from His hand

Here on the riverbank He will never leave

The day broke and I found the crown of your head under my hand

In what worlds were you I wondered

Where in the gold worlds did you wander

While parrots scolded themselves in the neem trees and the warm where

    my body had been

Rose into cold air

In the new light I could see your head, all gold, under my hand

In a new light your gold head

And it fell away

It fell away here

I will carry here back with me, she thought

I will bring it back with me

Under my hand invisible through customs in some cavity

No head will attach itself to my hand

I will find no head, ever, under my hand

Here will never leave, it will be everywhere with me

43   IN SPARE RELIEF

The dead ones are the pretty ones, said Lily,

with space, quiet, the occasional guide or guard, their gods

graceful and monochrome in niche

or in this narrative band of soft stone

all pavilion and demons, as in the poems.

Ruins like this are where they were, you can feel

how it was when they were here and real, how solemn

and clear it must have been.

                                 It wasn't like this

at all, said Chaz, looking up from his monograph.

(He was doing a post-doc in Chennai.) This was all

multi-colored and gaudy, as the great gateways are today

at Tiruvannamalai, Varadarajaperumal,

and Kailasanatha.

                    Right, she said.

Names that mimic those carved epic

artificially-colored clusterfucks overhead,

architectural comic books, all

claustrophobic and panic.

I need pale light and god as spare relief

for the India I've decided on, that I will need

to fall back on later,

false as it may be, will have been.

44   SARASWATI

Look at this one

said Dan,

thumbing

through a discarded

god calendar.

Completely white.

Four arms: book, beads,

canteen, guitar.

Rides a swan.

Distinguished by an absence

of jewels or color. Owns:

language, intelligence, song.

Consort to Brahma.

(The bland god, right, the guy

with no temples or stories?)

No, wait.

She's also a river.

Was a river.

Still a river but

with no water.

Go figure.

Either a metaphor or

what we've been after,

said George, putting the kettle on.

A Nadia, or Joanne.

45   SUNDAY MORNING

Early in the morning when it was yet dark she had gone back to the clinic

to bring Blake his clothes and they said he'd been discharged

he wasn't there so she went back and woke Simon and Peter

who came and up they went past the desk to the ward

but where he had lain only a small pile of T-shirt and sheet

and two orderlies each with good English

yes we had just been calling and promptly the Embassy gentleman

came as per instructed. Get Andrew and Nadia, said Peter and left,

but Sarah moved not. Then at the doorway

a tall man in white with no name

on his lab coat: *Who are you looking for? Why are you crying?*

She said, There could be steps right here, going down to some river.

My friend was not clay and glitter not an image of some orange god

not a version or bizarre incarnation of smudged attributes not something

you people bow to and chant at and throw your food and savings and shirts

this is he, is he, is not that, we refuse

to dance in some street-crush of half-naked hawkers and then throw him

at some astrologer's perfect moment into some clogged estuary,

she said, spilling everything onto the cracked tile.

Later, she thought he said *Sarah*, putting his mace, spear, and trident down on a chair, and came over to her, standing just out of reach.

46   BLAKE GOES HOME

Had it been a fiction, his refusals

and hard-won denials, each with its thread;

had his brute adherence to a bad translation,

his matted hair and cracked skin been a fiction;

had the burning ground, with its holy well, its annual

harvest of illumination and offal

been a fiction; had the holy men

hawking black words, oil, woodpiles

and the answer he'd come for been a fiction then she

would not have to answer, not have to step

into this blunt sunlight here on the tarmac

to accept from this Embassy Attaché

Blake's ashes, the fact of them.

(On her hospital window sill

a faded photo of a young man

and truck, a clay bird, mug,

and strung beads: cock-eyed still life

of hierophany and fragment

aslant, provenance unclear but

brought from home.)

Friends and strangers come.

They place before the child a tray

of objects—sacred and profane, familiar

from his prior life or not.

By what and whom he chooses,

by how he left.

48   THE INVISIBLE RIVER

I like it when you visit. The nurses leave us alone.

It's good that you keep coming back sharing

two stories at the same time. Did you find

the invisible river you wrote about? The one that was a music goddess too?

You and Andrew were so impatient for some beyond

that well I don't recall but might

it then be clear. For that you needed crows

and the smoky lane. Tied these to a tree and keep looking.

Not a sudden incoherence but the third strand of the story-braid,

that was visible but now is not,

tuning itself at the edge of this intricate carpet

as the opaque amethyst of evening

quiets the street noise and peacocks.

49   HAD SHE

Had she stayed

Had she not stepped up

Into the train that carried them down

From the hills to the plane

Home through Rangoon and Vientiane

She would know that

What *kailāsaranashiva*

chandramoulīphanīndramātāmukutī

zalālīkārunyasindhubhavadukhahārī

thujavīnashambomajakonatārī

In the cripple's mouth after he spat

At them, at the standing boxcars,

Means is

O Lord Shiva on Mount Kailash

Moon-Jeweled,   Serpent-Crowned

Ocean of Mercy,   Remover of Delusion,

Protect me   I surrender

Her head rolled away from my hand.

The sheet went white.

I have walked with broken feet, Mother,

from Never-Forsaken to here.

Lo, I have brought you the river, I said,

grandly, letting it pour

out of the high white ceiling through her hair.

Listen and I will tell you some of what I am.

Only the greatest parts, because there is no end to me.

Of rivers I am Ganges, Kaveri, Godavari, and thus

I am every river.

Of celestial musicians I am wind through pine.

Of trees I am the banyan.

Of snow I am silence and expanse.

Of the Himalaya I am the unnamed peaks.

Of the Vedas I am the omitted verses.

Of things that do not move I am indifference,

Of radiant spirits, amnesia,

Of prayers, the placenta.

Among things that purify I am sex or sacrifice.

I am those syllables that ignite.

Among those who watch in silence

I am the woman at the well,

Among those who watch in darkness the owl,

Among those who watch in daylight your mother

At the edge of the playground.

I fear nothing.

poring over the smudged in all this.

Blue-skinned bong-bearing

six-armed rat-riding jackal leaching

into one lotus-edged scene after another.

What. A few more

falling out as everything went

two-dimensional and the shimmering stopped.

Right before our eyes. The frame shifted.

Scenes and conversations have to be changed.

Past and present. Tense. Always tense.

53 KUMBH MELA, ALLAHABAD

So we drank the local palm wine, said Cindy,

trying to explain it all to Alison, later, in Houston,

and there were so many of us there looking

and like we all wanted to go to this Mela,

it was such a famous festival with millions of people

none of whom we had ever been but then

Blake got sick and everything

was suddenly really scary so we stayed in Goa.

Nevertheless, I think that was it. I do.

The relinquished festival, with its invisible

third river. What we might. After Blake's funeral the *Hindu*

had photos of trampled pilgrims and an ash-smeared

leper dancing his feet off.

54 YEARS LATER, SINGAPORE

In the evenings it's gods in the mirrors, bronze

and heavily-armed: Glocks, camo, Marlboros, Ray-Bans

the distinguishing iconography of the highly-muscular.

All these stories, she thought, and not

a riveting past life or parable in sight.

Let me go over this again for you

here at the Long Bar:

compared to that moment in Durga's shrine,

when in the dark we swore,

no Buffalo Demon stepping down

from an unmarked chopper matters.

Parvati flew off to pick up little Skanda from school.

Shiva was still at the agency with the other creatives

working on a cold front and a river system.

What would I tell these kids? Look carefully

at what offers protection. Stick together.

Scorn not the luminous tedium.

He pauses to erase a province.

From the corner office everything's in order.

The daughter of the Himalaya

is steadfast, beautiful, and a great mother.

On his desk a bronze of themselves, done

nine hundred years ago and now in a private collection.

56   WHERE IT WAS

Bearing jasmine we visit and revisit where the gods have been.

Where they have been they are close.

Geography's all body parts: That jagged ridge?

Remnants of demon spine. Temples founded

where Krishna made his flute, where each hacked-off gobbet

of Shiva's bright cock fell to earth. And our own

roadside hierophanies: vivid, life-altering, gorgeous.

Remember the man who sold silk, red wedding saris

splayed up against the wall, where we haggled

for a length of raw black to wrap our Tarot?

Where we came upon nothing between us, nothing

that like a glittering cobra had risen out of the earth and lay there,

all invisible coiled filigree on the wood floor?

Who will build there?

Sunset. The man's gibberish by the river.

Nadia's assertion. The Embassy visit.

Blake's death. Andrew's letter.

Supplementary or constituent?

Nadia's circumlocution. The albino calf.

The Embassy's warning. Blake's meditations.

The ash-smeared ascetics at the river.

Sarah's sister's letter. Nadia's lie.

Consecutive or causal? Dawn

Over the river. Andrew's abrupt departure.

The crows and banyan. The buffalo carcass. Jane's

Brother. The Embassy's folder.

Blake's illness. The man's

Incomprehensible blessing. Noon.

Andrew's letter. Narrative metalepsis:

What should Sarah tell her mother?

58   REASONS II

The marsh is full now, with the tide's glittering bounty

and this one atemporal heron.

That was never the reason,

Ben said, once, after long silence, as if turning away from us,

on horseback, more darkness ahead

but somewhere, surely, the city.

By now the whole trip

with its randy sub-plots and gods is of waning interest

and the late afternoon pulls itself, like our travelers, toward something

far ahead

but known only from texts, and still, even now, our role in it all unclear.

The bullock carts and tin-sellers in the choking street

only a spicy paste that, folded into a betel leaf,

is just reminiscent? Someone, surely,

remembers the canals and canyons carved out for us,

that our children imagine as they play up under the eaves,

as I write this down. I should offer a new one

and ride on, looking hard and ahead.

You're all exploration and production, said Andrew,

hunting what's compressed, pre-historic,

difficult of access, waiting to be brought to the surface and lit.

Not Exxon maybe but nonetheless

the upstream activities of an extractive multinational,

perspective long-term and global, damage

minor and local.

        Downstream,

above the refinery's skein of pipelines and cracking towers

a tall crane unfolds herself gracefully

back into a square of paper, pale yellow

on one side, lined on the other.

60 HAVING BEEN BACK FOR SOME TIME

Geoff tanned and just back from Goa once proclaimed

the beach scene at Calengute including Edwina and the Divine

Lili Whoever from Cologne unchanged. Fully in flow

we had dismissed it, all signed on to

you can't walk twice into the same. Nevertheless

this morning on the ice-bound river stalked

by black pines along the blank-white ridge,

not that this is the same river, your breath coiled in air

forms the Tamil word for *fig*.

61   THEOPHANY, BANGALORE

Demonstrating clearly cross-platform capabilities supporting the tier three help desk that guarantee the seamless migration envisioned by developers supporting the testing environment and strategic leverage toward cost-savings that are inevitable but not on the bleeding edge of the expense curve. Coffees in the atrium debating potential market share, penetration, saturation and speed-to-market, real-time data-aggregation, barriers to entry and opinions on competing technologies as force-multiplier or disruption in line with the morning's bullet points. To one side, surrounded by koi-filled meanders pretending to be rivers, a customer-facing four-armed bronze dances the universe toward an inflection point.

Om svāhā Shiva, muttered Andrew, daunted by sudden and comprehensive access to recovered but previously unmined data.

62   ENVOI

Everything I would share with you—prayer, bracelets,

dipthong, payroll, and pearl, maybe not in that order—

lies in the sun on the far bank. It's good to keep coming back

in those moments when you dare to look.

Watch the gulls. Two of them are always there,

radiant, dangerous, without flare or fondness.

Walk away. Now. While you can.

That's what I told them. As if her story was a seed

from which we learned nothing at the time or now,

that grew into revision, incineration, into what

a million ascetics splashing in a river seek.

63   LATER

Later I remembered looking up at our window

that could never have opened out

onto mornings thick with frangipani and dung-fire,

nor offered, in the middle distance, a view

of the old banyan by the well,

whose branch-threads, reaching down,

each one imagining itself the core of a new forest,

are adorned with small shreds

of sere cloth printed with prayers

or the hand-written pleas of the soldier's wife,

who, as we were told upon our arrival,

buried her bracelets one afternoon

and then walked, behind her dark eyes,

toward the banks of the river.

In that life, Ananda, I was the soldier.

NOTES

"3 The Jeweled Deer"
This jeweled deer is unrelated to those of Sir Thomas Wyatt ["Whoso List to Hunt"] and Petrarch [#190]. He is the demon Maricha of the *Ramayana* who, at the command of Ravana, demon King of Lanka, turned himself into a jeweled deer to lure the noble but exiled Rama (an avatar of Vishnu) away from the wilderness hut he shared with his beautiful wife, Sita. Ravana's abduction of Sita, and the ensuing war of Rama and the monkeys against Ravana and Lanka, constitute the major action of the epic.

"8 The First Evening, On the Way Back to the Hostel."
Anekashastrahasta is a Sanskrit name of the Goddess as Parvati. It means "possessor of many hand weapons."

"15 Mother II"
The text here draws on various translations of the Sanskrit *Devīmāhātmya*, Chs. 2.2-3.42

"19 Varanasi I"
The text in italics is drawn from the *Kūrma Purāna*, 1.29.22-54, tr. Dimmitt & Buitenen, *Classical Hindu Mythology: A Reader in the Sanskrit Purānas*, Philadelphia: Temple University Press, 1978. 330. The "Varanasi" poems also draw on "The Wanderings of Bhairava as the Supreme Beggar," Stella Kramrisch, *The Presence of Siva,* Princeton, NJ: Princeton University Press, 1981. 287-300.

"24 The Leper on the Bus"
Lines in the poems are drawn from translations of the *Katha Upanishad*, §3-4.

"29 Kali Meditation"
The poem is loosely based on the *Karālava danām ghoram muktakeśīm caturbhujām,* a piece of the *Kālī Tantra*, translated from a Bengali text by Rachel Fell McDermott. The text is a *dhyāna*, a text used for visualization during meditation. McDermott, Rachel Fell. *Singing the Goddess: Poems to Kālī and Uma from Bengal.* New York: Oxford University press, 2001. p. 9.

"30 One Afternoon Sarah Gets Lost in the Street of Butchers/ *The Goddess Durga Promises Blessings*"
The lines in italics are drawn from translations of the *Devimahatmya*, Ch. 12.26-29.

"45 Sunday Morning"
The poem draws on, and includes some phrases from the *Bible* (King James Version), John 20:1-18.

"51 Kali Answers Arjuna's Question"
The poem draws on translations of *Bhagavad Gita*, X. 17-42, in which Krishna, as charioteer, responds to Arjuna.

"63 Later"
Ananda was a much-loved disciple of the Buddha. Upon attaining enlightenment, the Buddha remembered all his past lives, and used "birth stories" [Jataka tales] from those lives as a vehicle for teaching the dharma. Many of these tales are explicitly addressed to Ananda. *The Jataka: Stories of the Buddha's Former Births.* E. B. Cowell, Ed. Robert Chalmers, Trans. London: Pali Text Society, 1895.

ACKNOWLEDGMENTS

I am grateful to the editors of the following publications, in which some of these poems first appeared:

The Beloit Poetry Journal, The Cortland Review, Little Star, The New England Review, The New Orleans Review Online, Poetry Daily, Provincetown Arts, and *Talisman.*

I also want to express my gratitude:

to Chip Loomis, my husband, and to our boys, Sam and William, for the weeks they spent visiting my India in 2005, and for their subsequent patience and support;

to my mother, who immediately recognized Gisèle, whom we met at Dipti's fruit juice stand behind the YMCA hostel in Mumbai in 1973;

to Heather McHugh, who blessed some early drafts and convinced me to keep going;

to Maeve Kinkead, J. J. Penna, Alicia Jo Rabins, Maggie Schwed, and Abby Wender, whose feedback on these poems was invaluable—they are this book's godparents;

to Martha Rhodes, who believed in this work way before I even knew what it was; and

to Bridget Bell, Clarissa Long, Ryan Murphy, Laura Swearingen-Steadwell, and everyone else at Four Way Books for their assistance in bringing these poems to readers.

Elizabeth T. Gray Jr. is a poet, translator, and corporate consultant. She has published translations from classical and contemporary Persian, and is currently collaborating on the translation of a Tibeto-Mongolian oral folk epic. She was the founding CEO/Managing Partner of Conflict Management Inc. and Alliance Management Partners LLC, consulting firms that assisted global corporations and governments form, manage, and repair complex inter-organizational alliances. She has a B. A. and J. D. from Harvard University and an M.F.A. from Warren Wilson College. www.elizabethtgrayjr.com.

Publication of this book was made possible by grants and donations. We are also grateful to those individuals who participated in our 2014 Build a Book Program. They are:

Nickie Albert
Michele Albright
Whitney Armstrong
Jan Bender-Zanoni
Juanita Brunk
Ryan George
Michelle Gillett
Elizabeth Green
Dr. Lauri Grossman
Martin Haugh
Nathaniel Hutner
Lee Jenkins
Ryan Johnson
Joy Katz
Neal Kawesch
Brett Fletcher Lauer & Gretchen Scott
David Lee
Daniel Levin
Howard Levy
Owen Lewis
Paul Lisicky
Maija Makinen
Aubrie Marrin
Malia Mason
Catherine McArthur
Nathan McClain
Michael Morse
Chessy Normile
Rebecca Okrent
Eileen Pollack

Barbara Preminger
Kevin Prufer
Soraya Shalforoosh
Alice St. Claire-Long
Megan Staffel
Marjorie & Lew Tesser
Boris Thomas
William Wenthe